Lego Bricktales

The Complete Guide & Walkthrough with
Tips &Tricks

LEGO Bricktales Medieval Level Walkthrough and Builds

The Medieval is the third world that players can visit in LEGO Bricktales. In this level, the citizens of the kingdom is stricken by an illness and it is up to the players to find out what's causing them to get sick, as well as finding the cure.

In this guide, we will talk about the Medieval level in LEGO Bricktales, how to solve the builds and the puzzles, and locate the collectibles within the level.

Medieval Walkthrough and Builds

You arrive within the walls of a castle. Head to the castle and speak to the King. Then, go to the Chief of Guard standing at the gate and he will tell you to get a sword before you can venture out. You then head to the Industrious Smith, but he's out of coal and you need to go to the Charburner.

However, the Charburner is sick and needs your help getting coal by fixing the transport cart. The build shown in the examples below are simple, if not the simplest solutions, but you can change the build as you like, so long as it passes the objective.

Medieval Build #1 – Coal Cart

For the coal cart, you need to place the tall 2×2 bricks along the sides first, then place the thinner blocks on both ends. Make sure that the slopes are facing down inwards to catch all the coals. You also need to use the 2×3 plates to make 2 layers of flooring inside the cart to prevent the coals from getting stuck when being poured. Do not make the wall facing the dumping spot too high, or the coals will overshoot. Once done, get your sword forged by the smith and head back to the guard.

Medieval Build #2 – Stone Bridge

With the sword on hand, you will then be able to venture outside the castle. You will then need to build a stone bridge to cross to the other side. Make use of the arches to be able to reach both ends of the gap.

Explore the area and head to the northwest path where you will pass by the Wizard Imposter who needs help with his rabbits.

Enter the cave that leads to the Dragon's lair. Head to the east end and follow the path down into the lower level. When you arrive at a dead end, head to the west and you will be able to get your whip to get the other collectibles in the area. Head back up a level and climb up the ladders to arrive at the exit. Head further back up and talk to the Dragon and it will require you to gather gold before it lets you enter the Skill Temple.

Open the gate near the lair to get a shortcut back to the forest. You then need to talk to several of the people in this level to do some odd-jobs in exchange for some gold. First off, visit the Scatty Wizard Weniglin.

Medieval Build #3 – Sitting Perch

Head back to the place where you first arrived at the forest and head east to arrive at the Wizard's house. You'll meet up with the Scatty Wizard Weniglin and he needs your help to create a sitting perch for his owl.

You can start the build by stinging the 1×1 tall studs and create a platform low enough so that the owl can fit or steer clear of the upper base. Then, if you place the owl to the side, you will have to balance the perch by adding more blocks to the other side. You can use the meter on the upper right corner to see if the perch is unbalanced. Once done, you will be rewarded with a gold coin.

Medieval Build #4 – Well

Head back to the castle and talk to the Well-Builder. You will then have to build a well. Build the walls of the well first, and then put the long plates across the walls so that the main bucket can be placed in the middle. Then finish the well off with whatever blocks you want.

Medieval Build #5 – Chicken Fence

Next, head to the Chicken Keeper and she will ask you to build a fence for her chickens. You can make just a very simple fence out of a few bricks as long as it prevents the chicken from escaping.

Medieval Build #6 – Balcony

Next, talk to the Minstrel and he asks you to make a balcony for the princess. Mind the filler marks on this build; it's better to use the studded plates than the flat or tall ones on the spots where you need to fill. Make sure to support and fasten it properly to the wall, too.

Medieval Build #7 – Crenellations

Head inside the castle and go up the stairs to the left to meet up with the Architect. She will then ask you to create crenellations for the walls. Any crenellation design will do as long as you cover the marked areas properly.

Medieval Build #8 – Throne

Then, head to the Jester in the King's chamber and she will ask you to create the King's throne. Do any design that you like, just make sure that the seat is above the floor and the crown is above the seat.

Medieval Build #9 – King's Statue

Finally, talk to the Jester again and she will give you the key to the Treasury. I here you will need to find the King's statue and some artificial flowers. Once done, head back to the King's chamber and build the statue scene for the king. Any design will do as long as there are at least 10 bricks, and the King's statue is in it. Once you have collected your gold coin from the Jester, head back to the Dragon.

The Dragon will then let you inside the Skill Temple. In here, you will learn the Water skill which allows you to wash off any dirt and fill up any receptacle with water. Grab the skill in the middle of the temple to start. Since it is a Skill Temple, you will only be able to use one skill at a time between the Smash and the Water skills.

To solve the Skill Temple, follow these steps:

Switch to the Water skill and head down the ladder to the north

Use the first bridge wheel to turn the bridge and then switch to Smash to destroy any crates

Go down the ladder again to get the Suspicious Potion, then switch to Water

Head back up and fill the receptacle with water to make the water rise

Use the wheel to open a gate hiding the second bridge wheel

Use the second bridge wheel to get to the other side

Switch up to Smash to destroy the crates

Switch back to Water to wash the lever that lowers down the gate

Climb back up and fill the receptacle to raise the water level again, allowing you to exit

Before heading out, use the Water and Smash skills to reach the chest at the back of the room to get some drumsticks.

Head back to the castle and use your Water skill to cure the sick people. Then, report to the King and he will require you to find the culprit of the poisoning. Head to the Wizard's house to find out that the Wizard was the culprit all along. Go back to the King and he will tell you to help the Chef. Talk to the Chef at the castle hall and you will be asked to repair the banquet table.

Medieval Build #10 – Banquet Table

For the banquet table, we recommend to use 1×1 studs for each of the leg, followed by the inverted slope. This way, the long plates will be able to sit on top of the legs. Make sure the sandwich the middle part on both the top and bottom sides as the turkey can be quite heavy.

After this build, the kingdom will have a banquet and then you will get another Happiness Crystal.

Head back to the Theme Park to rebuild the next attraction. This build is not part of the Medieval level's completion, but it unlocks the next level.

Medieval Animal Collectibles

In the Medieval level, there are a total of 20 animals to be collected. 15 of them can be found within the first run through the level, while the other 5 will require a revisit once the necessary abilities to reach them have been acquired. Check out our complete guide for the animal locations in All Animal Locations in Medieval Level LEGO Bricktales.

All Animal Locations in Medieval Level LEGO Bricktales

There are plenty of animals that can be collected within the Medieval level of LEGO Bricktales and while some can be spotted easily, others require more efforts in searching and some specialized skills in order to obtain them.

In this guide, we will talk about where to find all the animal collectibles in the Medieval level in LEGO Bricktales.

Medieval Animal Locations

In the Medieval level, there are a total of 20 animals to be collected. 15 of them can be found within the first run through the level, while the other 5 will require a revisit once the necessary abilities to reach them have been acquired.

In Medieval, you will find four (4) of each type of animal, with the Rabbit as the main animal for the level needed by the Wizard Imposter.

Check out our LEGO Bricktales Medieval Level Walkthrough and Builds guide to know how to complete the level.

Bird – found in the starting area, south.

Hermit Crab – found in the starting area, near the chicken coop.

Chameleon – found in the castle, stairs to the left.

Rabbit – found in the forest area, just past the Wizard Imposter.

Ladybug – found in the first room of the Dragon's Lair.

Chameleon – found in the first room of the Dragon's Lair, underground passageway.

Hermit Crab – found in the first room of the Dragon's Lair, after getting the whip underground, trace your steps back and use it to reach a ledge.

Bird – found in the upper outdoor level of the Dragon's Lair.

Ladybug – found in the castle's treasury.

Bird – found in the castle's treasury, upper floor.

Rabbit – found in the castle's treasury, south passageway.

Ladybug – found in the forest area, west corner, clean away the dirt at the base of the ladder.

Rabbit – found in the Wizard's house, clean up the dirt using the Water skill.

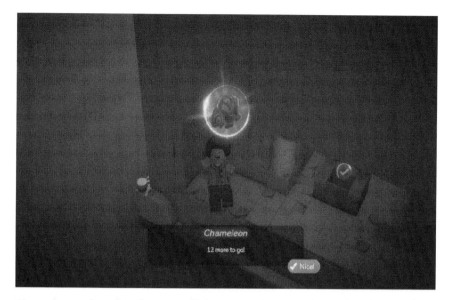

Chameleon – found in the Wizard's house, in the closed chamber that can be opened using the wheel.

Ladybug – found in the castle, clean up the dirt using the Water skill

Repeat Run Medieval Animal Collectibles

These are animals that can only be obtained when you have unlocked the advanced skills. You can revisit the level and use your new skills to find the other animals.

Hermit Crab – requires the Hover skill; in the middle of the forest where the first entrance to the Dragon's Lair is, use the Dimension skill to reveal a rail. Then use Hover to get to the other end to reach the hermit crab.

Rabbit – requires the Electricity skill; in the Dragon's Lair, go to the middle of the room and head down the stairs to see a teleport pad. Use Electricity to move into a room where the rabbit can be found.

Chameleon – requires the Hover skill; go behind the cart of the Charburner to find a rail. Use Hover to reach the other side of the map. Then, use the Whip to climb higher where the Chameleon is.

Hermit Crab – requires the Electricity skill; in the Castle Hall, use Electricity to teleport on top of a ledge where the hermit crab is.

Bird – requires the Hover skill; found in the starting/town area, go near the exit leading to the forest and use Dimension to reveal a rail. Use hover to go up the gate, then use Dimension to reveal the wheel. Turn the wheel to open the gate on the main castle, then make your way to the top by going inside the castle and taking the stairs and exiting through the door. Finally, go through the door to get the bird.

Medieval Chests

There are a total of 13 chests to be found within the Medieval level. Not all of them can be found within the first run as you will need to acquire additional abilities to reach them. Check out our guide for the chest locations in All Chest Locations in Medieval Level LEGO Bricktales.

Medieval Shop

There are 10 different items on sale in Boo's Medieval Shop and they all count towards the level's completion when purchased. You will need a total of 250 drumsticks to purchase everything in the shop.

Medieval Bricks – 100 drumsticks

White – 15 drumsticks

Dark Stone Grey – 15 drumsticks

Silver Metallic – 15 drumsticks

Bright Blue – 15 drumsticks

Jester's Shirt – 22 drumsticks

Jester's Pants – 12 drumsticks

Dragon Knight Chainmail – 20 drumsticks

Jester's Cap – 18 drumsticks

Dragon Knight Helmet – 18 drumsticks

All Chest Locations in Medieval Level LEGO Bricktales

Treasure Chests are scattered all across the Medieval level in LEGO Bricktales. Unlike the usual treasure chests that often carry lots of gold and valuable stuff, these treasure chests contain things that aren't usually what one would expect, but they are still considered as valuable currencies in their respective worlds.

In this guide, we will talk about all the chest locations in the Medieval level of LEGO Bricktales and share tips on how to get to them.

Medieval Chest Locations

There are a total of 13 chests to be found within the Medieval level. Not all of them can be found within the first run as you will need to acquire additional abilities to reach them.

Check out our LEGO Bricktales Medieval Level Walkthrough and Builds guide to know how to complete the level.

10 Drumsticks – found in the starting area.

50 Drumsticks – found in the first forest area, after building the stone bridge, take the ladder and follow the northwest path until you see the Wizard Imposter.

10 Drumsticks – found in the next forest area, via the path past the Wizard Imposter.

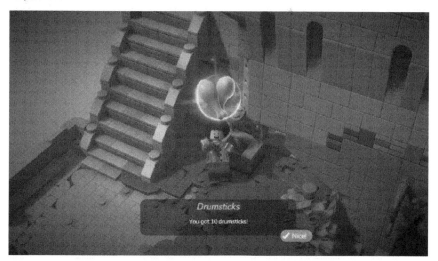

10 Drumsticks – found in the upper outdoor level of the Dragon's Lair.

10 Drumsticks – found inside the Wizard's House.

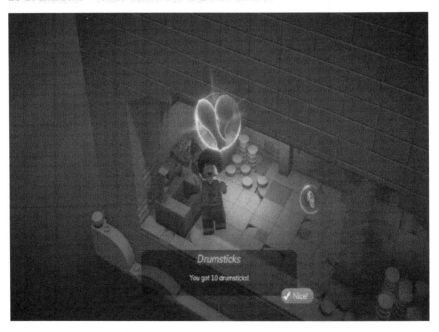

10 Drumsticks – found in the castle's treasury, use a whip to go down a level.

50 Drumsticks – found in the Skill Temple, wash the smash skill switcher and smash the crates.

10 Drumsticks – found in the Wizard's house, in the closed chamber that can be opened using the wheel.

10 Drumsticks – found in the castle's treasury, clean the lever using the Water skill and then use it to lower down the chest.

50 Drumsticks – requires the Electricity skill; inside the Dragon's Lair, use the Whip to climb the ledge near the lower entrance to reach the wheel. Then, turn the wheel to open a gate. Climb the ladders nearby to reach the teleport pad and use Electricity. Pull the lever to lower the chest in the center of the room then make your way back to the chest.

10 Drumsticks – requires the Electricity and Hover skills; in the Dragon's lair, go to the middle of the room and then down into the stairs. Follow the path going to the west until you reach a dead end. Use the Hover skill to go to the higher ledge and then use the wheel to lower a gate. Go to the east corner and where the broken bridge is. Use the Water skill to clean the dirt off the teleport pad on the other side. Then, retrace your steps back to the teleporter you just passed and use Electricity. Make your way up the stairs and the ladder to reach the chest.

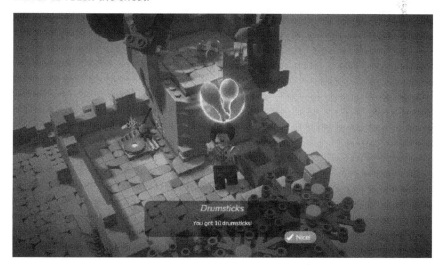

10 Drumstick – requires the Electricity and Hover skills; in the forest, make your way to where the Dragon is, then clean the dirt using Water to reveal a hover rail. Use Hover to reach the other side where a wheel is. Use the wheel to lower a gate, then make your way back to where the gate was to find a teleport pad. Use Electricity to get on top of the castle where the chest is.

10 Drumstick – requires the Electricity skill; in the King's Chamber, make your way to the treasury room and exit through the other passageway back into the King's Chamber. Then, use Water to clear the dirt off the teleport pad. Head back to the main King's Chamber and use the teleport pad on the corner to reach the chest.

LEGO Bricktales: All Caribbean Building Puzzle Solutions

The fifth world in LEGO Bricktales is a Caribbean island filled with quirky pirates. There are a lot of problems to be solved on the island, and many will take expert building skills. You've made it this far, but the Caribbean has several challenges that might require you to tear down your whole build and start over if anything is off.

If piratical precision is causing problems, this guide will provide step-by-step instructions for creating functional builds. It may not be a treasure map, but it's far less cryptic and still leads to a Happiness Crystal!

As with the other levels, most of the puzzles in LEGO Bricktales' Caribbean world have more than one solution. All the builds in this guide have been tested and proven to work, but you might find other functional solutions as well.

How To Build The Pig Cart

The pirates don't have horses, so they use pigs to pull wagons full of goods around the island... or rather, they would if they had any wagons.

Start by placing both of the largest plates on the base and connecting them to the pigs using rounded pieces.

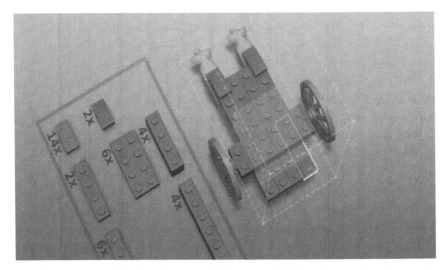

Attach four of the smaller thin plates to the underside of the cart, so that each has two pegs extending toward the rear. Make sure they clear the cargo area.

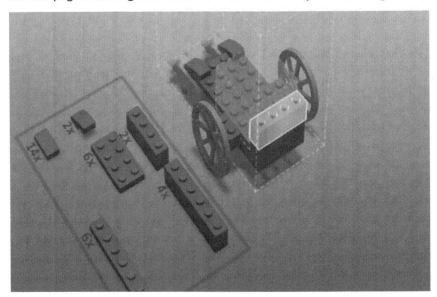

Stack a pair of four-peg bricks on the rearmost part of the wagon to form the backstop, then add a plate between it and the main part of the wagon to even out the floor.

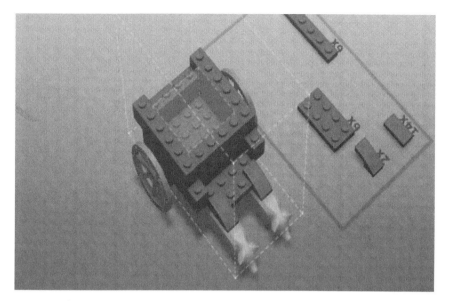

Stack bricks on the remaining sides of the cart to fully enclose the cargo area without putting any pieces inside it.

Fill the gap in the backstop with two-by-four plates so that all the wagon's walls are the same height.

Cover the top of the cart with smooth plates to give it a finished look, then run your simulation - it should hold all the coconuts with ease!

How To Build The Raft

To reach Boo's shop and several quest items, you'll need to build a raft on the beach.

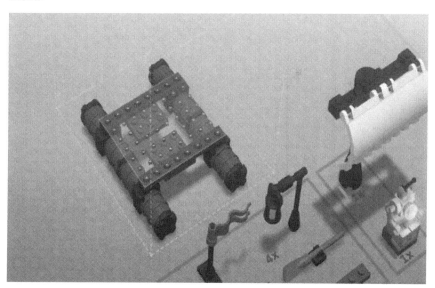

To start, connect the two logs with thin brown pieces at each end. The pieces will touch, but won't be connected until you put something above or below them.

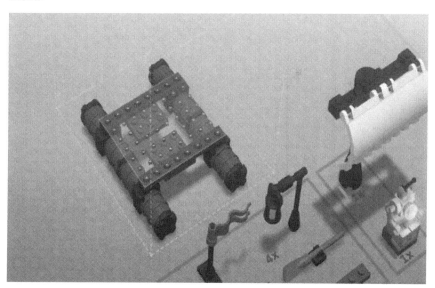

Use your entire allotment of light-brown three-peg plates to start building a support structure underneath the raft. Again, they won't connect just yet, and the raft will be asymmetrical.

Use the longest available plates to connect the support pieces perpendicularly, then use the dark-brown three-peg plates to connect them from the top.

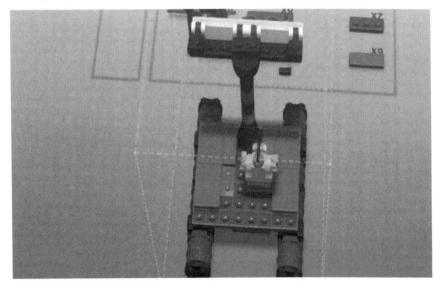

Place the sail and the test robot wherever you want, then start covering the top of the raft with smooth plates.

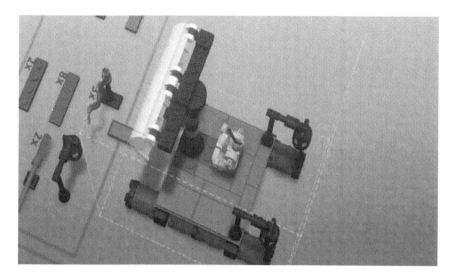

As long as the top of the raft is entirely covered, it doesn't matter which kinds of pieces you use. Lanterns, oars, and flags can all be used to give your raft some character!

How To Build The Fishing Pier

Not only does the fisherwoman's pier need to reach deeper water, but it also needs to have all the amenities for a perfect day of angling.

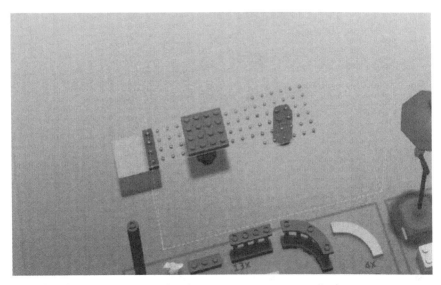

Start by placing a pair of two-by-four plates on the central pillar.

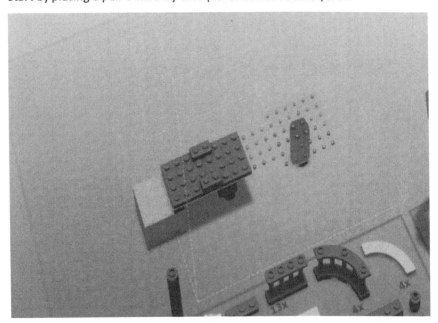

Use a pair of connectors to add another plate extending toward the shore, then place a fourth plate at the dock's starting point.

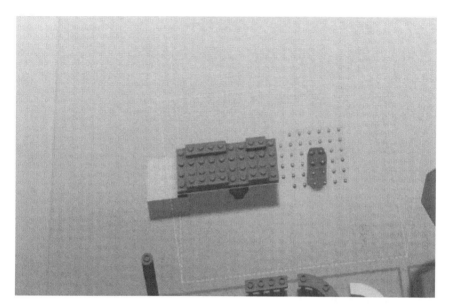

Continue using plates and connectors to extend the pier and hold it together.

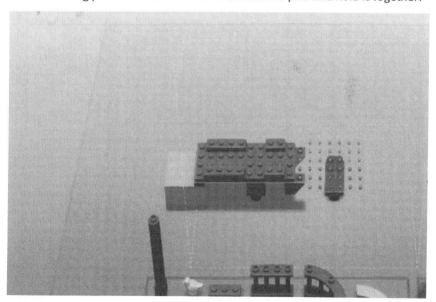

Just before the dock widens, place two inverted wedges underneath to connect the next set of pieces.

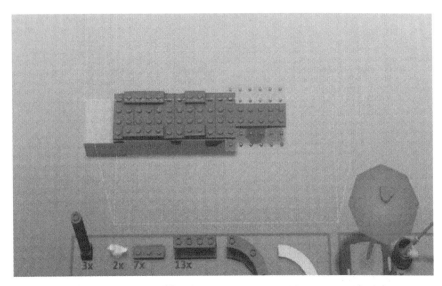

Put a long plate on the far pillar, then place corner plates on each of the inverted wedges.

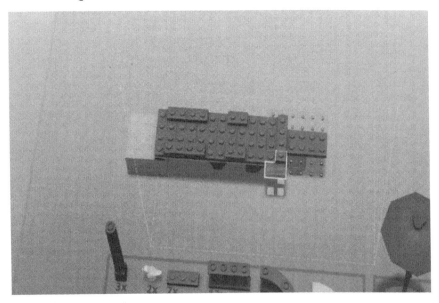

Cross the plate with a pair of connectors, then hang corner pieces underneath the sides curving the back toward the shore.

Place connectors over the newest corner pieces so that you can hang plates underneath them to complete the basic dock structure.

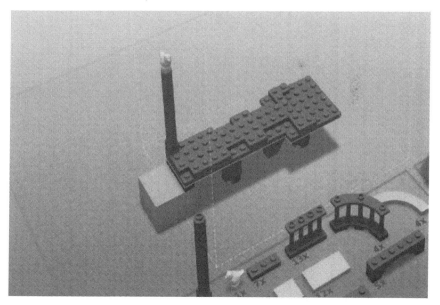

Cover the middle path with plates to even out the surface and connect the plates beneath.

The center path has to remain clear, so you can extend platforms out to the sides to place the tackle box and umbrella.

As it turns out, having two poles at the start of the pier as shown in the image above will impede you later on. If you place a pole on the nearest corner to the piece stockpile, it will block you from being able to speak with the fisherwoman when she moves later in the story. Luckily, you can always remove the pole at that time!

How To Build The Caribbean Bridge

Unlike the previous feats of engineering in the game, the bridge in the pirate's hideout is fairly straightforward.

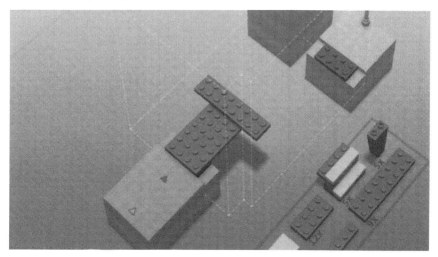

Start by using three long rectangular plates to make a thick T-shape extending from the start point. This way, you have the makings of a path to both flags.

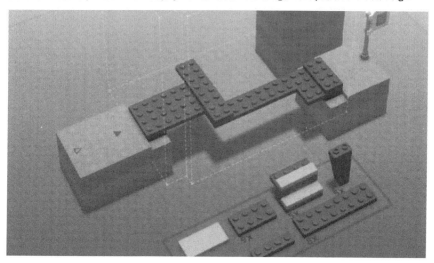

Hang another long plate under the right side of the T, extending toward the blue flag. Place smaller plates to connect it to the anchor point as shown above.

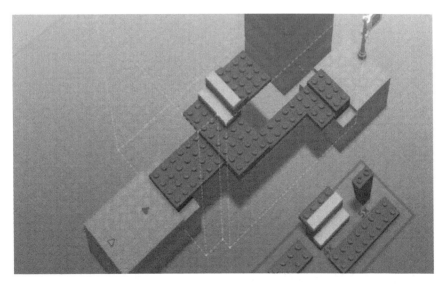

Put a set of stairs on the left side of the T, with plates hanging underneath to create a platform.

Use more stairs and plates to reach the green flag. With your main structure in place, the next step is to reinforce it.

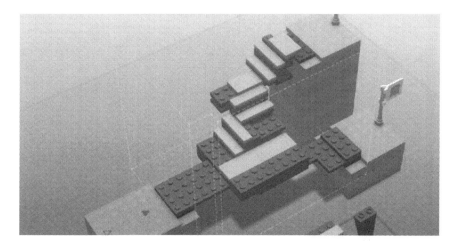

Connect pieces to any cracks that you see. Try to do so from underneath wherever possible so as not to accidentally block the test robot's path.

If you miss a weak point and the bridge breaks, simply reinforce it and run your simulation again!

How To Build The Parrot Perch

Once you've recovered the missing parrot, it's time to build a perch for the pirates' impressive collection of avian specimens!

Begin by attaching a red inverted wedge to the anchor. Hang two regular brown wedges underneath it to create a splitter.

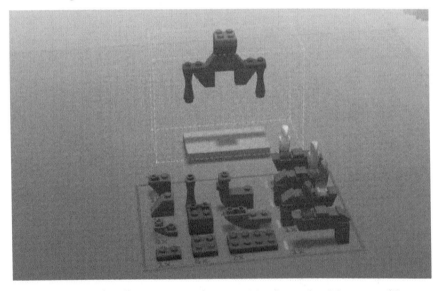

Hang an inverted wedge underneath each of the far ends of the assembly.

Using a red connector on top of each inverted wedge, attach a cone hanging down.

Attach a second cone to each side, so that they hang almost all the way to the floor.

Using curved pieces, extend the assembly to the rear so that you can place two of the parrots behind the anchor. One will need to be slightly higher than the other.

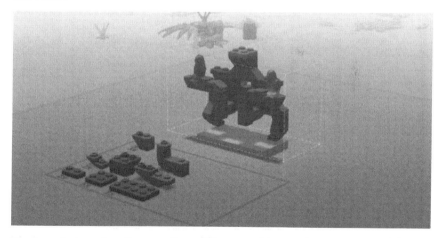

The inverted wedges from earlier still have usable attachment points. Build toward the front to create space for the remaining parrots.

If the perch leans too far in one direction when you run your simulation, add bricks to the other side to counterbalance it.

How To Build The Lookout Tower Stairs

With limited pieces, several obstacles, and considerable height to climb, the lookout tower is one of the most challenging vertical builds in the game.

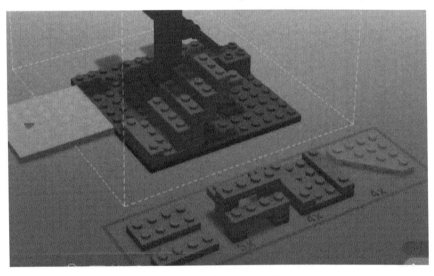

Placement is important from the very beginning. First, put a square piece in the corner to the right of the starting point. Stack two sets of stairs on top of it to reach the first support platform.

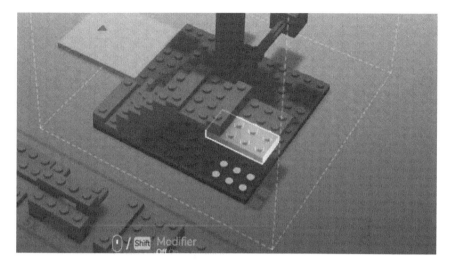

Use another square to connect the stairs to the support platform.

Next, attach a pair of two-by-four plates to the square from underneath. They will hang just barely over the edge of the ground plate, but they'll still be within the bounds of the build area.

Stack two thin plates at the end of the platform to create a support beam, then place a corner piece on top of the structure as shown above.

Add two sets of stairs, ascending toward the second platform. They won't quite reach, but with a thin plate attached to the end they allow the platform itself to be used as a step up!

If you're worried about the stairs breaking, place a two-by-four plate under the support platform. You can connect it to the stairs from below.

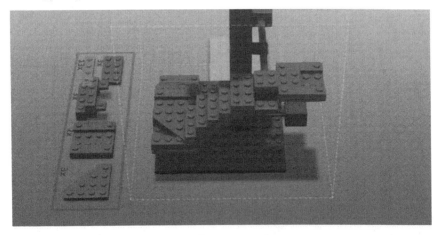

Using a two-by-four plate as a connector, attach a square piece to the far side of the support platform. Be sure not to stack anything else on top of the connector by the stairs, as otherwise it will become too tall to climb.

Add a layer of plates on top of the square to give the structure more height, then place a corner piece on top.

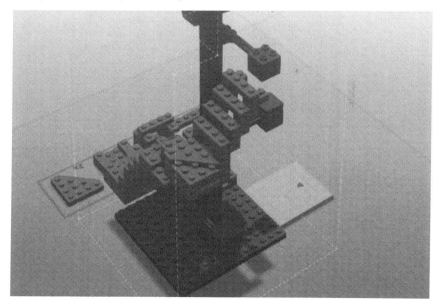

Attach the next pair of stairs, leading up to the third support platform. It will come in just a little lower and farther away than is ideal, but that's easily fixed.

Use a plate to connect the stairs to the underside of the support platform. Next, stack a thin plate at the top of the stairs to give them sufficient height to reach the platform.

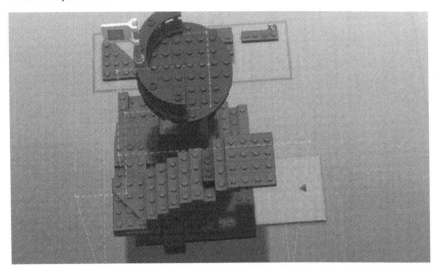

Attach a two-by-four plate to the support platform, covering only the far side so that the dark brown part can still be used as a step.

Next, attach four thin plates to the end, creating a square.

Stack a corner piece on top of your new platform, followed by your last stairs and one of the square pieces.

Fill the gap in the square with thin plates.

Use your remaining plates to attach the assembly to the lookout tower. Run your simulation, and make any adjustments necessary to prevent breakage or to keep the robot from getting stuck.

How To Build The Rainwater Collector

The cook's rainwater collector can be frustrating, because it has to be built perfectly. If even a single drop of rain doesn't make it into the barrel, the game won't consider the challenge complete. It can be helpful to run a few simulations at the start just to see where the raindrops land.

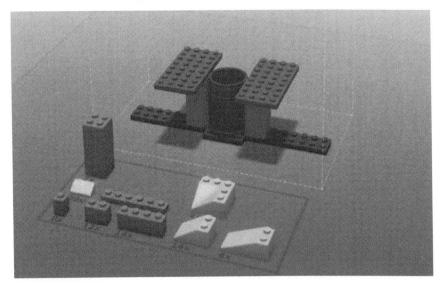

Start by placing a pillar immediately to either side of the barrel. Place two squares on each as shown above to create your main support platforms.

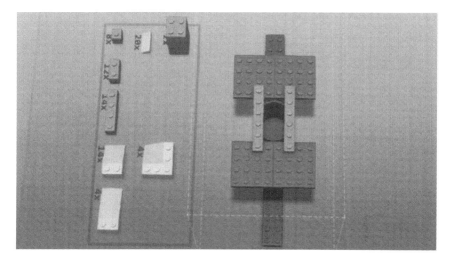

Connect the squares with the two long, thin plates at your disposal. Place them so that they slightly cover two sides of the barrel. The goal is to minimize the chance that any raindrops will bounce off of the barrel's rim.

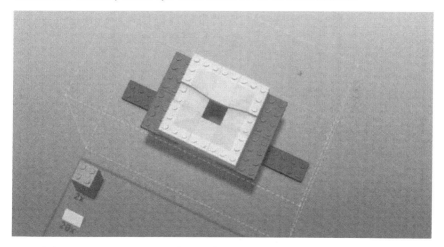

Attach the four corner pieces with a short wedge in between, all sloping toward the center of the barrel. Two of the wedges will be slightly lower than the rest of the assembly, but that's okay.

Ensure the hole over the barrel is as small as possible. If it's too big, raindrops will miss the barrel!

Place a small slope on top of the two short wedges to help direct raindrops toward the center.

Next, add a pillar to either side of the main structure. Place bricks on top to extend the assembly in both directions, but make sure that it's leaning more toward the piece stockpile. This is because more raindrops fall in that area than the space behind the collector.

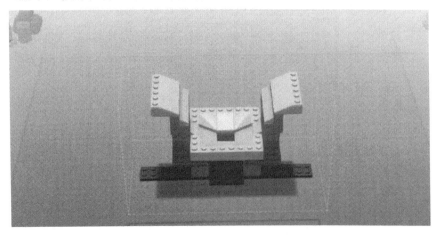

Build up the leftmost and rightmost sides with another set of bricks, then add a set of wedges to each. Place slopes directly below the wedges as shown above to continue feeding into the barrel.

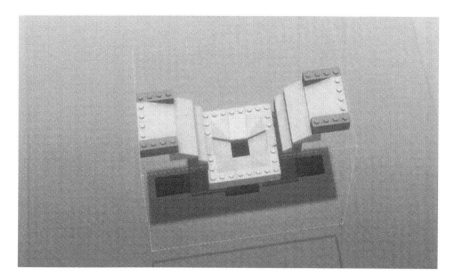

Attach a pair of long wedges to the middle of each side - both should touch the outer edge of the build area. Place a brick on either side of these wedges.

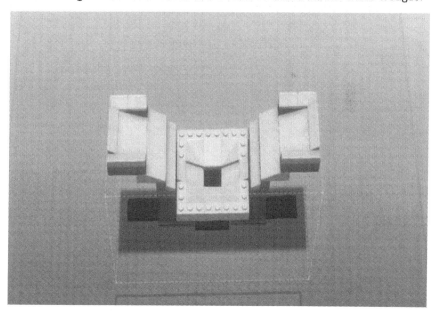

Cover the flat tops of the structure with sloping pieces. You don't need to do so around the edge of the main basin, just the highest parts.

With the main structure complete, run a simulation. Chances are that a handful of raindrops still won't make it into the barrel.

Watch where they land and add slopes to the structure specifically to get those raindrops back on track. Use the above image as an example.

If it looks like you caught everything but the game still isn't letting you complete the challenge, move the camera around.

Look for raindrops that may have gotten stuck on the way down in a spot you couldn't see before, or bounced off of a wall somewhere.

You should have enough leftover pieces to catch any stray raindrops - in our playthrough, there were three. Once all the rain is in the barrel you can move on.

How To Build The Cargo Lift

In a secret cave, you'll need to repair an old cargo lift to reach the legendary pirate ship. This challenge requires you to not only build a platform capable of holding weight, but to distribute that weight evenly and keep the lift balanced.

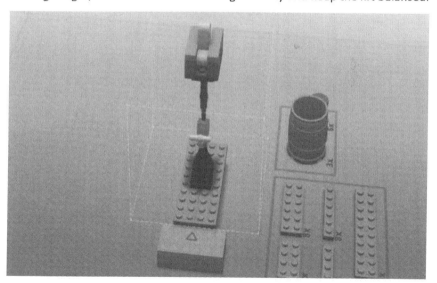

Start by using two of the longest plates available to create a path from the starting point to the lever in the middle.

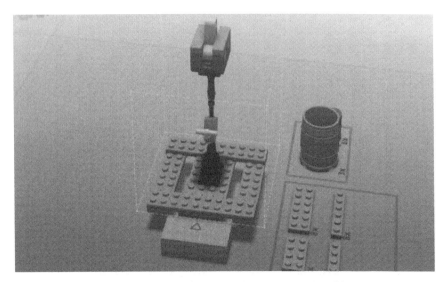

Use the remaining long plates to build a square around the lift.

Next, use two-by-four plates to fill in the gaps to the left and right of the lift.

Place bricks in front of the switch to create a handy step up!

Now, the challenge is to distribute the weight of the nine barrels evenly across the platform. The configuration pictured above is proven to work. You can also add plates to the platform on the lighter side to incrementally add weight instead of shifting barrels.

How To Build The Gangplank

It's fitting that the final challenge in the game is a bridge. This time, however, you'll be building vertically, then dropping the bridge down!

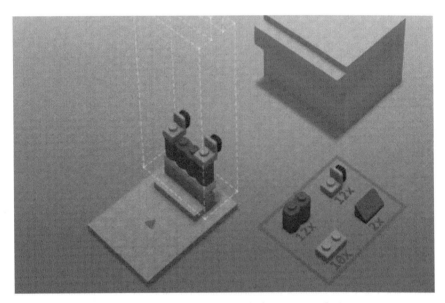

Place a pair of the rounded brown pieces side-by-side on the base plate. Attach one of the irregular gray pieces to each side, with the black part facing the flag.

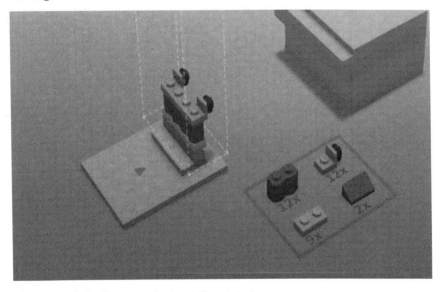

Place one of the flat gray pieces at the center.

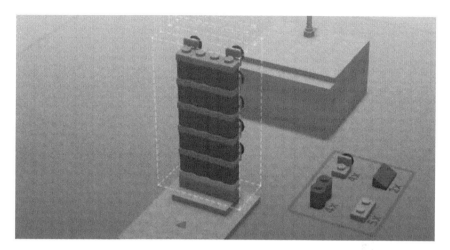

Repeat the above steps four more times, building the structure taller until you reach the point where the build area narrows.

Place the next set of rounded pieces as normal, but only cover the top with a pair of small flat plates.

Place the two triangular pieces at the very top of the assembly, with the slanted edges facing toward the flag.

When you run your simulation, the gangplank should hold together when it lands, allowing the test robot to cross. Board the ship and return to the pirates' hideout in style!

Made in the USA
Middletown, DE
31 October 2023

41716548R00035